THE UNVEILED KING

THE UNVEILED KING

ASHER COOPER

DEDICATION

This book of poetry is dedicated to the many teachers and supporters who have helped steer my life in the direction that it is today.

I'm forever grateful for their wisdom. Above the many, I would like to select a few that I believe are worthy of highlighting:

Dr. Myles Munroe's teachings have been a pillar of strength for me over the years and a beacon of hope to millions around the world. May his name continue to be even greater in death.

To Apostle Benjamin Smith, who is affectionately known as 'Papa', a man who carries the mantle of many great leaders that have gone before us. May you continue to be a voice that echoes through the government halls of nations.

To Dr. Dave Burrows, the ruffneck Pastor who always made time out of his busy schedule just to meet with me. You made me feel so valued, and for that, I'm eternally grateful.

To Dr. Susan J Wallace, who reignited my fervour for poetry in me. May Bahamian history never forget you. I surely will not!

To Ian Rolle, one whom I've always admired and who has been an encouragement to me over the years. May Grand Bahama reap the rewards of your excellent leadership.

To my siblings; Dudley Jr., Esther, Jephthae, Elijah, and Lydia. Thank you for your unwavering support over the years. It means so much to me. You are irreplaceable in my eyes. Last but not least, to my parents Dudley Sr. and Etta Cooper who made a sacrifice for my siblings and me, my love for you has no end.

And to the countless millions who desire to become the best version of themselves, it is the desire for myself also. May these poems bring refreshment to your soul, light to your eyes, and truth to your heart. My hope is that the King and Queen will be unveiled in you!

TO THE READER

This anthology of poems is comprised of inspirational and empowering truths. You will not only be uplifted when you read this book but you will also be directed onto the path of purposeful living. I encourage you to read these poems no less than three times, for you will not get the best understanding of the poem in its first reading.

In every poem that I have written, I've used a unique choice of words to express myself. You're getting my heart and emotions in each line. As a philosophical poet, my job is to get you to gingerly think about your life but most importantly for you to take a proactive course of action if needed.

This book will take you on a journey from self-imprisonment to self-actualisation and towards the path of liberty. You will realise that the only restriction to your success is you.

Enjoy!

TABLE OF CONTENTS

PART 1: UNVEILED SECRETS OF LIFE

IF THERE WAS NO REASON TO FEAR

If there was no reason to fear,
Could you imagine what we could do?
The goals that we would have,
And the dreams that we would pursue?
If there was no reason to fear,
What could we achieve?
There would be no reason to doubt,
Because we would always believe!
If there was no reason to fear,
Like eagles we would soar,
Anything would be possible,
And torment would be no more.
If there was no reason to fear,
We would strive for the very best,
And have all that our heart desires,
Requiring nothing less.
If there was no reason to fear,

We would talk like a king,
Have the attitude of a lion
Because of our strong self-esteem.
If there was no reason to fear,
Poverty would be no more.
We would find
That we have the power in our minds
To unlock any closed door,
If there was no reason to fear!

LINE OF SIGNIFICANCE

"We would find that we have the power in our minds to unlock any closed door, if there was no reason to fear".

1. What do you think the writer meant based on reading the line of significance?
2. What fear do you currently have that could be causing you to limit yourself?

GOD'S GIFT TO MAN

How can I describe a woman
Who's a blessing to a man?
First, she is filled with wisdom,
That only God can understand;
She has the kind of ability
That the sun has on the earth.
An obstacle is her fortune,
You can never calculate her worth.
She is more precious than diamonds,
Than the rarest you can find.
Her thoughts are of so much value,
Like there are oil wells running through her mind.
So, men, if you see such a woman,
Hold her with so much love,
Because you didn't find this lady;
She was given by the Father above!

LINE OF SIGNIFICANCE

—∞∞∞—

"Her thoughts are of so much value like there are oil wells running through her mind".

1. In the poem *God's Gift to Man,* what do you think the poet meant based on reading the line of significance above?
2. In your own words, explain which line stood out to you and why.

WHAT IS FREEDOM

Freedom. What is it?
Is it something where we are free from chains?
Or is it where we are free in our brains?
You tell me!
What is freedom?
Because I'm not sure.
How can we accept freedom from chains
But nothing more?
What is freedom?
I'm so confused;
In the 21st century,
We accept mental abuse.
What is freedom?
When you don't control your time
And ruefully go to a 9–5
With depressed hatred inside.
What is Freedom?
Will you let me know?
The answer to my question

May give me a ray of hope,
Because when I look into my mental scope,
The definition of freedom can only be a joke.
We are:
Consumers but not creators;
Parasites but not producers;
Smart but not wise;
Good-looking with no substance inside.
Is this freedom?
Or is this something we have accepted?
We question our governments.
But don't we also need to be inspected?
What is freedom?
Answer the question.
Truth must be confronted,
Before he exposes you to the lesson.

What is freedom?

LINE OF SIGNIFICANCE

—⸺—

"Truth must be confronted before he exposes you to the lesson".

1. What do you think the writer meant based on reading the line of significance above?
2. Briefly, in your own words, explain what freedom means to you.

NUGGET OF TRUTH
THINGS THAT WE ENJOY

———∞———

We enjoy:
Laws we never created,
Medicine we didn't research,
Cars we didn't design,
Homes we never built,
Freedom we didn't fight for,
Grace we didn't die for,
A father's love we don't deserve.

What will we enjoy from you?

WHAT WE CANNOT
LIVE WITHOUT

The king wants it,
The queen wants it,
Politicians want it,
And even you want it.
What is it that you want?
What is it that your heart desires?
It's so intense
That it heats, then singes,
For commitment is what it requires.
To some, it's a mystery;
To others, a complicated case.
It comforts the broken,
Fights for the weak,
And confronts evil to the face.
It entices and seduces,
But completely refuses

To stand on par with anything else;
Yet we don't mind having it for ourselves.
It's cold when it needs to be,
But warms up almost instantly.
We can't live without it,
Graceful as a dove;
Yes, we'll go crazy
If we don't have love.

LINE OF SIGNIFICANCE

⸺◈⸺

"To some, it's a mystery; to others, a complicated case".

1. Based on the poem, why did the writer compare love to being a mystery to some and a complicated case to others?
2. In your own words, please explain why love matters to you.

SOMETHING THAT
WE ALL NEED

It takes virtue to attract her,
Strength to hold her,
Knowledge to keep her,
Wisdom to preserve her,
For she was the solace of kings;
She stood the test of time.
Every great achievement,
She was there;
One of a kind.

No project was too great
That she did not help to do;
Just give her time,
And she will shine;
Success is in her clues,
For it's a joy to meet her,

A beacon of light to nations.
I speak of none,
But only one:
Her name is PATIENCE!

LINE OF SIGNIFICANCE

———∞∞∞———

"Every great achievement, she was there; one of a kind".

1. What do you believe the writer meant based on reading the line of significance above?
2. Why do you think having patience is important?

THE VALUE OF TIME

What would you do with your time?
Because life seems so short.
We only have a few days
To run through the maze
Despite what you've been taught.
Your time is a priceless treasure,
More valuable than silver and gold.
You can lose wealth and regain it again,
But what will you do when you're old?
For we all have a limit
To be here on this earth.
It doesn't matter how rich you are,
You will still be covered with dirt.

LINE OF SIGNIFICANCE

———∞∞∞———

"We only have a few days to run through the maze".

1. What do you believe the poet meant based on reading the line of significance above?
2. How do you plan to make maximum use of your time?

NUGGET OF TRUTH
FASCINATION OF THE ANT

If you trap him one way, He'll go another to get to his destination.

He's not great in personal strength, But he's great in numbers.

You can find him in your yard and in palaces.

And if you look down and see him, No question he's on an assignment!

UNTIL

Until has no boundaries;
Perseverance is akin to his name,
For thinking 'Until' isn't good enough,
You would be the one to blame.
For Until can see the future;
He can see it from afar.
Although Until has failures,
He delights in wearing his scars.
Until can outstrip talent,
Intelligence has nothing on him,
For Until would never ever give up.
He would fight until he wins.

LINE OF SIGNIFICANCE

—◦◦◦—

"Until can outstrip talent".

1. In your own words, explain what you believe the writer meant from reading the line of significance above?
2. What have you learnt from 'Until' that you can apply to your life?

MIND BATTLE

———∞———

Change is always constant,
For we must change with the time.
Before there is victory,
The battle must be won in the mind.
Failure is never final;
What matters is what you believe,
For we must have the resolve to win,
Before there is a need to succeed.

LINE OF SIGNIFICANCE

———⚬⚬⚬———

"For we must have the resolve to win before there is a need to succeed".

1. Based on the poem, why do you think we must first have a resolve to win before we can succeed?
2. Do you agree that change is always constant? If so, why?

POWER OF TRUTH

God always had a plan
For the entire human race.
If men ever fell,
He knew what he would do to put us back in place.
In dominion, we were created;
Dressed in splendour and royalty,
But somewhere along the line,
We became confined,
So, we ignored who we should be.
Therefore, this was his dilemma:
If man ever ate the fruit,
He could never go too far
Without food, water, and truth.

LINE OF SIGNIFICANCE

"But somewhere along the line, we became con-
fined, so we ignored who we should be".

1. What do you think the writer meant in the
   line of significance shown above?
2. Why do you think knowing the truth is
   important?

NUGGET OF TRUTH
WHAT MUST BE REVEALED

Three things that cannot be hidden for long and the fourth, the most powerful, are:

- The sun
- The stars
- The moon
- The truth

THE DIFFERENCE BETWEEN CHICKENS AND EAGLES

Chickens and eagles are both birds.
However, I should make this clear:
One you can spot walking the floor,
The other you'll see in the air.

LINE OF SIGNIFICANCE

"Chicken and eagles are both birds".

1. Based on the statement "Chickens and eagles are both birds", list five things that they have in common.
2. List five things that they do not have in common.

PART 2: UNVEILED MYSTERIES OF DECEPTION

BACKBITER BETH

Mary had a friend
Whom she loved with all her heart.
She promised Beth only in death
Would they ever be torn apart.
But Beth never loved Mary;
She used her in every way.
Wherever they both went,
Mary had to pay.
Beth was so toxic;
She had only one friend.
But Mary didn't care
Despite being aware
What poison does in the end.
One night, as Mary slept,
An assassin entered her home.
The man took his time
To make sure she was alone.
He then entered her room;
As he aimed towards her head,

Mary, scared and startled,
Started to cry as she wet her bed.
Her final words to him
That seemed like a mystery
"How did you get inside"?
He then replied,
"Beth gave me your keys".
POW.

———∞∞∞———

To be continued.

LINE OF SIGNIFICANCE

———∞∞∞———

"Mary didn't care despite being aware what poison does in the end".

1. What do you think the writer meant based on reading the line of significance above?
2. What can you do to ensure that you avoid people like Beth?

POISON

Your mind is your greatest treasure.
Guard it as best as you can,
For ignorance seeks
To prey on the weak;
He delights in destroying the man.
Therefore, he must be conquered.
He is enemy number one!
He'll spread poison to your mind and soul,
Then kill your only son.

LINE OF SIGNIFICANCE

"For ignorance seeks to prey on the weak".

1. What is your interpretation of the line,, "For ignorance seeks to prey on the weak"?
2. In your own words, explain how you will guard your mind against ignorance.

THE DANGER OF SAYING "I QUIT"

The world gives us what we ask for,
But we must present our case.
Although we are filled with treasures,
Many let it go to waste.
For the greatest danger is not
The one who lies in the pit,
But tragedy finds
the mentally blind,
And those who love saying "I quit"!

LINE OF SIGNIFICANCE

———〰———

"But tragedy finds the mentally blind, and those who love saying "I quit".

1. What do you think the poet meant based on reading the line of significance shown above?
2. How has quitting something in the past restricted your progress?

NUGGET OF TRUTH
THE DESTROYER

❧❧❧

Ignorance doesn't care what you discover, as long as you
don't discover yourself.

Will you follow the rules of ignorance?

BACKBITER BETH: PART 2

Mary opened her eyes.
She couldn't believe, To her surprise,
She was still alive.
No feeling of pain,
No blood in sight
Except sobering in fear,
Because the gunman stood near.
Mary pleaded, "Take my wallet and my keys,
You can have anything,
But don't kill me, please.
You see, I'm too young;
Too young to die!
I've got dreams and goals".
"Shut up", he replied.
"Your friend is your enemy
Who wanted you dead".
The more he talked,
The more she became scared.
"You should fear Beth more than me.

You will not die today, as you can see.
Call it luck or count it a blessing;
You now have another chance to learn your lesson".

"Everyone you like
May not like you.
So test your friends;
Once or twice won't do".
Before he departed,
The final words he said,
"Choose your friends wisely",
as if he cared.
What a night to escape death;
The only thing left to do
Is to confront Beth.

———◦○◦○◦———

To be continued.

LINE OF SIGNIFICANCE

꧁

"So test your friends; once or twice won't do".

1. Why do you think the assassin told Mary to test her friends?
2. If you were in Mary's shoes, what do you believe would be the best way to deal with this issue?

NO MORE RELIGION

One of the greatest destructions of man
Is this vain sadist.
Not only have we held her to a standard,
It's her that the world praises.
First, we created her,
Next, we inflated her twisted ego,
Then she turned and took dominion
Over the minds of the people.
For she has captured more lives,
Leading us to an unknown path,
And if we fail to comply with her,
She insists on displaying her wrath.
She says, "Religion is freedom",
But I'm locked up with chains,
Sitting in a dungeon cell.
Is this what freedom means?
I'm now disgusted by her.
In fact, I hate religion!

How could you reward me for being good
By putting me in a prison?

Whether Hindu, Muslim, or atheist,
Or anything from that crazy list,
Which separates and discriminates.
And worst of all, eliminates.
I now cancel my silence
For now, I take a stand.
For I will do anything To ensure that she is banned.
No more religion!

LINE OF SIGNIFICANCE

—❧—

"One of the greatest destructions of man is this vain sadist".

1. Why does the writer refer to religion as one of the greatest destructions of man?
2. If God never made religion, or if religion is manmade, what can we do to get closer to God without the various forms of religion?

ARE WE THERE?

It hurts my heart to question
The conscience of our people.
But are we there?
To a place where
We are threatened by no form of evil?
Bigotry, injustice, and religion,
To me, is old news.
But can we find a haven
That will arrest and suppress old feuds?
Gender equality,
Majority and minority,
Past conflicts
That questions our sovereignty.
We the people, united as one,
Have become a people
Divided by guns,
Divided by hate,
Divided by race,

Divided by creed,
Human needs and faith.

Are we there?
Or do we fear
To love someone?
We must treat them with care.
Perhaps it's just me;
The way that I see
The world that it is,
And what it needs to be:
A world of peace,
With joy and care,
Because my prayer is:
Together we'll get there.

LINE OF SIGNIFICANCE

⸎

"But can we find a haven that will arrest and sup-press old feuds"?

1. Based on the poem, what do you think the writer meant based on reading the line of significance above?
2. Which line of this poem stood out to you and why?

NUGGET OF TRUTH
THE HUMAN DILEMMA

We have:
Dads, not fathers;
Houses, not homes;
Procreators, not protectors;
Jobs, not work;
Skills, not gifts;
Sight, and not vision;
Fantasies, but not dreams;
Knowledge, but not truth;
People who are making no progress.

CHOICES

It's not whether one can,
It's a matter of whether one will.
You are the result of every choice;
You must pay your bill.
The decisions we make
Will help to shape our lives.
If you're wrong, it's a forlorn thorn
That goes as deep as a knife.
Therefore, let knowledge guide you,
As you go well on your way,
For we will live with every choice
As long there's night and day.

LINE OF SIGNIFICANCE

—⟨∞⟩—

"If you're wrong, it's a forlorn thorn that goes as deep as a
knife".

1. What do you think the writer meant from reading the line of significance above?
2. List five choices that you have made that you are proud of. Also, list five choices that you have regretted.

THE DANGER OF IGNORANCE

Nothing worthy of achieving
Comes without a fight.
Your mountain is your Goliath;
Conquer it with all your might.
We were born to be victorious,
Not to live life in defeat,
For at the door of our minds
Stands ignorance That keeps us weak.

LINE OF SIGNIFICANCE

꧁꧂

"For at the door of our minds, stands ignorance that keeps us weak".

1. What do you think the writer meant from reading the line of significance above?
2. How can you conquer your Goliath?

THE HOT-HEAD

How hot is the man
From whom temper takes no bribe?
His ego is full of arrogance,
And his anger won't subside.
His pain lies within
Only soon to realise
The hot-head man, I know,
Will regretfully claim his prize.

LINE OF SIGNIFICANCE

"The hot-head man, I know, will regretfully claim his prize".

1. Based on the poem, why do you think the hot-head man will regretfully claim his prize?
2. What should you do if you're confronted by someone with a temper?

NUGGET OF TRUTH
CLASH OF OPPOSITION

———∞———

Good vs. Evil
Skill vs. Gift
Courage vs. Fear
Light vs. Darkness
Heaven vs. Hell
Health vs. Illness
Opportunity vs. Limitations
Success vs. Failure

In life, we must pick a side in our pursuit of our destination. Most importantly, we must be cognizant of the ramifications that may ensue.

BACK BITER BETH: PART 3

As the man exits the door,
Mary wept uncontrollably,
"How could Beth do this to me"?
She said emotionally.
"After all the things I've done
For her over and over:
The clothes, the shoes, the jewels, and the Rover".
"How could Beth do this to me"?
"She owes me her own life.
When no one was there for her,
I was always there on sight.
I gave up my own time
To cater to her needs.
How could I be such a fool
Not to see that jealousy breeds?
I'm through with Beth!
Tonight, I could've been shot"!
She said, "I hope she goes to hell",
And that is where she rots.

Then Mary remembered,
Even though the man had a mask,
He had a heart on his hand.
The tattoo was clear,
Plus it read, *Beware!*
Could it be her school crush Stan?

To be continued.

LINE OF SIGNIFICANCE

⸺∞∞⸺

"How could I be such a fool not to see that jealousy breeds"?

1. What do you think Mary meant when she said, "How could I be such a fool not to see that jealousy breeds"?
2. Based on the series of Backbiter Beth poems, what have you learnt about Beth?

PART 3: UNVEILING THE HIDDEN TREASURE

WHO AM I?

Who am I?
Is a question many ask
With superficial answers
To such an important task.
Who am I?
Am I defined by my skin pigmentation?
Or professional occupation?
I wonder, is that all there is to me?
Perhaps deep inside
Lies treasure that hides,
And to discover who you are
Must be pursued diligently.
Our face says that we are fine,
Yet we are living, but not alive;
Working, but not fulfilled;
With sight, but still fully blind.

Who am I?
You must seek clues

Before truth unveils the news.
There's no reward without labour,
So do yourself a favour,
Look deep within your soul
And gather up the wealth of gold.
I am living proof!
Because I know who I am!
But I wonder, who are you?

LINE OF SIGNIFICANCE

—∽∞∾—

"Perhaps deep inside lies treasure that hides".

1. Based on this poem, can you identify some treasures that you believe hides?
2. List five things that you can do to further discover yourself.

THE UNKNOWN EAGLE

We were born to be eagles,
Destined to grace the sky:
If this statement is true,
Then can you tell me why
Many would rather be chickens
And live their lives in despair?
They would rather stay on the ground
Than with the Masters of the Air.

LINE OF SIGNIFICANCE

—∞∞∞—

"Many would rather be chickens and live their lives in despair".

1. What do you believe the poet meant based on your reading of the line of significance above?
2. List three things you can do to have an eagle mindset.

BORN TO SOAR

Should you leave your future to chance?
Why go through life without a plan?
For failure seeks to demand a dance
With the person who kisses his hand.
Opportunity needs preparation,
And strategy breathes success.
You were born to soar!
Not to walk the floor,
Nor live your life in a nest.

LINE OF SIGNIFICANCE

"For failure seeks to demand a dance with the person who kisses his hand".

1. What do you believe the poet meant from reading the line "Failure seeks to demand a dance with the person who kisses his hand"?
2. After reading this poem, why do you think it is important to plan?

NUGGET OF TRUTH
THE BEAUTY OF DIFFERENCE

———∞∞∞———

Difference is the:
Fuel for creativity,
The seed for growth,
The yeast for rising,
The weapon against tradition,
The key to significance,
The measure for true success,
The vitamin for a healthy organisation,
The machinery for results,
The anthem for a movement,
The beat to stir up disturbance,
The mark for no toleration,
The light that chases away darkness.

We value difference when we realise there's beauty
in being different.

THE LIGHT

The light becomes much valuable
During the hours of the night;
He exposes the weakness of darkness,
Driving him off in fright,
For we were born to shine
As brightly as can be.
You are the answer to your generation:
Without you,
How can others see?

LINE OF SIGNIFICANCE

"He exposes the weakness of darkness, driving him off in fright".

1. What is your interpretation of the line "He exposes the weakness of darkness, driving him off in fright"?
2. How can you be a light in your school or your community?

VISION CALL

What would life be like
If everyone lived with vision?
Imagine the progress we would have
And the quality of each decision.
We would pursue our purpose
And believe more in our dreams.
The mission of our lives
Would be nothing less but reign.
If you and I lived with vision,
Can you imagine the attitudes of our minds?
Plus, we would all find
That we are designed
To see even when blind.

LINE OF SIGNIFICANCE

"If you and I lived with vision, can you imagine the attitudes of our minds"?

1. What do you think the writer meant by the line of significance above?
2. Explain what vision means to you and why you believe having a vision is important?

UNVEILED KINGS

———∞∞———

Creativity is exposed in crisis,
And every obstacle can be a blessing.
Although we will make mistakes,
We are wired to learn the lesson,
For we're not created
To accept what failure brings.
We are born to rise
Like the sun in the sky.
Where's your crown?
We are unveiled kings.

LINE OF SIGNIFICANCE

—∞∞—

"We are wired to learn the lesson".

1. What is your interpretation of the phrase "We are wired to learn the lesson"?
2. Why do you think creativity is exposed in crisis?

NUGGET OF TRUTH
LEADERS CALL

We need lawyers,
We need preachers,
We need doctors,
We need teachers,
We need scientists,
But most importantly, true leaders.

MASTER MIND

Throughout my life
I've always thought less of me.
Instead of settling for greatness,
I chose mediocrity;
Never knew the world was determined
To give me whatever I asked.
I was tempted and willing,
But my request seemed much too large.
So, I accepted my plight.
Perhaps success wasn't for me.
Being guided by ignorance,
I went down the paths of misery.
Therefore, let this poem inspire you,
For you are one of a kind.
We must think highly of ourselves;
We're the masters of our minds!

LINE OF SIGNIFICANCE

"Being guided by ignorance, I went down the paths of misery".

1. What does the poet mean by this line of significance?
2. What does the line "We're the masters of our minds" mean to you?

THE PREREQUISITE
FOR SUCCESS

———⚬⚬⚬———

Wisdom is the virtue of the wise,
And diligence and patience are friends;
Success comes only after sacrifice,
For only then will you win.

LINE OF SIGNIFICANCE

———⊚⊚⊚———

"Wisdom is the virtue of the wise".

1. What is your interpretation of the phrase "Wisdom is the virtue of the wise"?
2. Please explain why sacrifice is important if you want to have success. What are you willing to sacrifice for your success?

NUGGET OF TRUTH
VALUE

Your difference enhances your uniqueness.
Your uniqueness expands your value.
Your value creates a demand.

DESTINY

All great achievements in life
Starts first in the mind;
It then grows into an idea,
But results require time.
We are born to become
All that we are destined to be.
For fear subsides
Because courage is alive
When you choose your own destiny.

LINE OF SIGNIFICANCE

"For fear subsides because courage is alive".

1. What is meant by the writer when he says, "Fear sub- sides because courage is alive"?
2. Recall three times in your life when you had to display courage.

THE WEALTH OF THE CEMETERY

We are filled with power;
Innate treasures are hidden inside.
For the greatest misfortune to life is this:
Cemeteries collect them when we die.
Here, you can find great wealth;
Wisdom lay in the carcass of minds.
There lie men with amazing vision
But chose to live frustrated and blind.

IN THE GRAVE COMMONLY LAY:
Princes who died as paupers,
Employees who were filled with business,
Free men who desired to be slaves,
Trailblazers who accepted the path fully paved.

FOR SHE IS RICH:
With poems that were never written,
Scripts that were never seen,

Songs that were left unrecorded,
And kings that never reigned!
In light of what has been said,
What will be your fate?
Because the grave is never satisfied,
She is looking for the next candidate!

WILL YOU ADD TO THE CEMETERIES'
WEALTH?

LINE OF SIGNIFICANCE

———

"There lie men with amazing vision but chose to live frustrated and blind".

1. What do you think the writer meant in the line of significance above?,"
2. Do you believe that the cemetery is the wealthiest place on earth? Give reasons to justify your answer.

NUGGET OF TRUTH
THE PARADOX

—∞∞∞—

We want:
Success without sacrifice,
Sacrifice without discipline,
Discipline without pain.

In order to have success, we must be willing to sacrifice, and the level of sacrifice produces discipline, which inevitably brings pain. There is no shortcut to true success.

ABOUT THE AUTHOR

Asher Cooper was born in the beautiful islands of The Bahamas, in the nation's second city of Grand Bahama. He is the second son of seven siblings born to Dudley and Etta Cooper.

Asher Cooper is a motivational speaker, businessman, and a Master Poet. He has spoken at a number of churches, schools, and professional clubs.

Currently, he sits on the Board of Directors at Progress Academy School. He was awarded a Competent Communicator Award from the Toastmasters International club where he served as Vice President of Public Relations.

He refers to himself as a truth dealer whereby his message of hope and truth transcends age, race, culture, creed, and country. He believes that we must never settle for mediocrity but rather settle for greatness!

Contact the Author:
Our current mission is to mitigate the illiteracy gap and encourage creative thinking through

life-changing poetry. Our goal is to disseminate this book throughout high schools and colleges. If you would like to help with this initiative, Asher Cooper can be contacted by: asher.n.cooper@gmail.com or asherthepoetphilosopher@gmail.com.

www.ingramcontent.com/pod-product-compliance
Lightning Source LLC
LaVergne TN
LVHW021408080426
835508LV00020B/2496